D1276433

Street Corner Majesty

David Harris

authorHOUSE®

AuthorHouse™
1663 Liberty Drive, Suite 200
Bloomington, IN 47403
www.authorhouse.com
Phone: 1-800-839-8640

© 2009 David Harris. All rights reserved.

No part of this book may be reproduced, stored in a retrieval system, or transmitted by any means without the written permission of the author.

First published by AuthorHouse 4/27/2009

ISBN: 978-1-4389-5593-3 (sc)

Library of Congress Control Number: 2009901350

Printed in the United States of America
Bloomington, Indiana

This book is printed on acid-free paper.

Book cover design by Kathy Keler.

This is book is dedicated to a few of my many muses...

Corinne Kennon-Harris
Marina Ioffe
Meredith Stewart

and to Jen McClurg and Ashley Goff
whose vision and support made this book possible.

A Brief Introduction

This is a book about a few years of my life- I chose to tell my story in poems as I lived through these experiences. The most interesting few years of my life began in Winter 2001, when I found myself living on the streets of Washington, DC, cold, lonely, hungry and scared.

After a couple of weeks on the streets, I met a lady, a veteran of homelessness, who told me about Miriam's Kitchen. Miriam's is a soup kitchen inside a church near downtown Washington, and it provided me with far more than meals- it was a place to go in the morning and escape the weather. I also found friends among the staff and volunteers there. The director at the time was Ruth Dickey, who also was a poet. Every Wednesday morning Ruth would lead a group of us in writing poems. I had written poetry many years before, but it was only because of Ruth's group (and others at Miriam's led by volunteers) that poetry became a part of my life again.

The group provided me with a network of friends among the other homeless poets; I considered Ruth a good friend as well. At each session, Ruth would give us each a topic to write about; we'd write for twenty minutes or so and then each of us read our poems to the group; after each of us shared, there would be comments from everyone- things often got really lively. Many of the poems in this book came from these groups.

Poetry gave me a way to express all my feelings and experiences on the streets; and when I escaped the streets, it gave me a way to share my joy.

My life on the streets was bleak in many ways but I had some very positive things going on in my life. I joined the speaker's bureau of the National Coalition for the Homeless- the NCH speaker's bureau is a group of people who have experienced homeless and speak to various groups about experiences. Being involved in this gave me another network of friends and a way to do something positive with my life; thousands of people have learned from my story. One result of this was my involvement with a Pilgrimage Service Center. Inside Church of the Pilgrims (PCUSA), The Pilgrimage is place where youth groups from around the country stay while they do service work around Washington. Our speaker's bureau gives talks there often. A few years ago, the staff of The Pilgrimage invited me lead some of the groups in written reflections about their experiences serving the needy. I lead the groups in ways I learned from groups. Many of the volunteers write beautiful poems and essays; many find these workshops very moving experiences. I often write along with the volunteers; some of the poems in this book are from these workshops.

I've been published in several poetry anthologies but I'm very excited to finally have a book of my own- it's been my dream for a long time. I hope you all enjoy my words- and learn from them, too.

-David Harris,December 19th, 2008

Table of Contents

Street Corner Majesty

Look at her-
she is regal
in her threadbare second-hand coat
and church-lady hat
garlanded with bright feathers,
the queen of her street corner.

She sweetly smiles and sings
for harried rush-hour passersby;
a few drop coins,
most glance away,
disgust, guilt, or a twinge of fear
stamped on their hardened faces.

A curious traveler
with a moment to kill
stops to chat, and discovers
she has a tale, a life
beneath the veneer
of city grime
and corrugated skin.

She is a mother;
her children are in places
of wealth and power;
one son's
precisely surgical hands
bear the power of life and death.

She is an artist;
she paints intricate portraits
of passersby who stop long enough
to be exposed for the camera of her eyes.

She is a lover;
a lonely man's fantasy
of silk, lace
and kisses raining down on him
like softly brushing feathers.

Twilight gently lands
on her corner of this earth;
she stands and trundles away
her rolling suitcase,
not bound for the alley where she lives
but for Paris in the spring
where she will pluck colorful blossoms
to adorn her crinkly hair.

May 8th, 2002

181

Strasburg, Harrisonburg, Staunton...

We tumble onto the road
from 66
and embark on a bright September journey
that begins with gentle rolling hills.
In spots, Earth's birth pangs are seen
as rocky scars on hillsides.
Soon, the terrain grows more rugged;
ridges and valleys
slide past our windows,
indifferent to our passage.

Lexington, Roanoke...

Little towns like postcards
(each with its white church steeple
and garland of sleepy clapboard houses)
are strung along the highway
like beads upon Virginia's necklace.
Meanwhile, gas, food, and lodging
are offered at every exit

Blacksburg, Christiansburg, Radford...

The New River unfurls its sleepy majesty;
serenely, she accepts our awe.
as we bear southwest,
the steep green shoulders of ancient mountains
guard our passage like gods of summer

Near Pulaski, a sudden cleansing shower
slows our progress;
we wait inside our steel cocoon
as nature bathes the rich black earth

Wytheville, Marion, Glade Spring, Abington...

The towns blend into fading southern memories
of tall tea glasses, rocking chairs on porches,
children running home in twilight
to mothers' strident calls

Bristol, Blountville, Kingsport...

Tennessee extends its welcome
with the absurdity of a giant guitar.
81 pours us onto another road
where soaring mountains invite us
to rise among them;
they send us a silent signal
that within them, we can find a home.

September 10th, 2001

Loving Ariel

I first met her
young, lonely, blue
and strange

the vision of her
was a solitary comfort
in turbulent adolescence

Pale, near translucent beauty
spoke to shadowy voices within me

she offered pearls
for me to see and touch
and cherish

Her voice, a sad insistent murmur
haunts me across the years
between my youth and my today

I hear her whispers
in shells pressed against my ear,
and in hot breezes bringing storms;
when storms lash across my earth
her voice threatens and commands,
and when she shows me
an instant flash of daylight
I imagine that is only she
who lets me see my landscape clearly...

Desire for her
flares and fades
inside me from time to time;
in bright times like today
passion for her is often forgotten

but when I wander in the dark,
my heart releases
an involuntary cry;
in my dark and desperate nights,
I cry for Ariel

-August 4th, 2001-

1957 Scene
(Starring John Birks Gillespie)

All ears
tingle
with anticipation

& then

the first sharp note
stabs the air
followed
by glittering arabesques

a brass horn dances

making the color

of childish giggles

the elegant ladies
in their feathered hats
stop & stare

the floor is alive
with
limber dancers
as they turn & twirl

a caramel girl,
in flowing skirt
of lavender

is tossed

somersaulting airborne

the horn cajoles & scolds

trampling the beat

[restless tick-tock
by the sweating drummer]

sounds soar
miles above the floor

a furious crescendo

enthralls the audience

then a final fanfare

drops the dancers
into humid heaps
& the king
of this outrageous scene

leaves the moment
with a golden smile
stunned applause
trails him
into the steamy New York night.

Who is this girl, Sabrina?

A sylph,

nymph,

bottle imp?

Bottle
  blonde

source of
  hard young heat
    I fear to touch.

She lounges across my daydreams,
looking bored.
Waterfall
of spun-gold hair
hangs lankly like a windowshade;
she is as
mundane
as last night's
fish & chips.
She's as exotic
as an aperitif, tinted flame red,
served in a tulip glass-
her taste
  bites the tongue.

Who is she?

She's the woman from flat 5A,
carrying her laundry
in a wicker basket
while cold morning rain

washes the yellow
from her hair.

She's a screamer in bed
in the prison of my fantasies;
she is a jade elephant
standing sentinel
on my bedside table
fending off
my loneliness.

Who is this girl, Sabrina?
She's torn
from page fifty-eight
of a glamour mag.
She wears
angry red
stiletto heels and a curve-fitting sheath
the color of blood.

In my dreams,
she strokes me to life,
and I forget the darkness
of these damp days.

The Girl In The Photograph

She sits on a beach
counting her shell collection
a smile of mystery
winks at you from her sepia face
at night, you sit alone with her

wishing

that she were here.

Upstairs, in your four-poster bed
a woman waits
alone.

There is no
smile of mystery
on her haggard face;
her hands speak of
mops and dirty dishes,
of children's runny noses,
of soiled diapers,
of a thousand evening
sips of sherry.

She is not
the girl in that photograph
in the frozen world
of that forgotten beach;
delicate curls
frame
her moon-shaped face;
a skirted swimsuit
[in the demure style
of 1956]

hugs

her gently rounded curves;
her smiling lips
seem poised
for a quick kiss

or a splash
of girlish laughter.

You spend your night alone

with her and mournful memories.

The woman in your wedding room
            lies still, drained from weeping.
        A wrinkled, faded hand
        reaches
        to click the lamp into darkness;
she knows, this night.
            she will sleep alone,
                that she has lost her love
to the girl
in that photograph
& both souls in that sleeping house
                are doomed
                to loneliness.

March 6th, 2002

Why she spells it "Erykah"

Big Technics woofers
wrap me in
soft womb
of her voice

I lie peaceful in
cocoon of sensuality

~her sound
purrs, sways, seduces,
  r e l a x e s~

I vibrate in tune

with the tender g r o w l

of her lowest

notes

she is
whole woman

.......*.......

[not one of these
stick-slender cardboard cuties
sticking fleshy walls of cleavage
in your face,
she covers herself
in voluminous silk,
knowing
m y s t e r y
is oh so sexy]

........*........

Even her name
is a sacred
incantation

E R Y K A H

to be whispered,
savored,
sipped

to be

immersed in

Big Technics speakers
bring the roar, the moan,
the hush
the heaven
of her
into my
trembling
body & soul

14 February 2002

Gift from Marina

Angels
   come in so many
      shapes
      & faces

Marina's face, seen by my eyes
      for one last time
         shines with light.

At our final meeting, she gave me gifts
      of confidence, and love

even as
   she gently scolded me
      she spoke in the voice
of the nurturing mother she will be,
of the powerful woman
      she is growing into.

Tomorrow, she graduates
      from four years
         among the lost & desperate,
spreading the gifts of her strength & compassion
      among those lost in darkness.

Over the meal we shared
I gathered her light & purity
      into my soul,

then I wandered here, slightly dazed, to write about her
once again;
the gleaming words that pour from me
      have escaped for now
The love she poured into me

is captured
deep within me
and when I need strength,
I will draw it from
Marina's gift
to me.

May 17th, 2002

Glow

She made me glow
this morning
with a few tender words
and an embrace

i walked for hours
in the glow she made

feet tripping lightly
along city sidewalks

eight lines of love
were her first poem
(because she missed me)

and the space inside me
that had been bleak and empty
was filled blazing light;
this morning,
she made me glow

February 19th, 2002

One Day In Winter

i return here
  in the midst of a normal day
          except
  i mourn;
    i'm broke & hungry
        and it's cold outside.

my friend,
      serene, my source of comfort
          when i mourn small things
                    sits in rare tears;
          her only words to me,
            "a friend just died."

i sit on the sidelines
    feeling useless;
        my gift for words deserts me.
        meanwhile, she continues
        to work, to function, to plan
        in midst of a normal day.

her simple words
      hit like bricks
        "a friend just died"
    and i'm reminded
        of the fathomless reservoir of love within her
        and inside, i cry for her
        but outward, offer
        only
        useless silence.

i'll leave here tonight
    broke, hungry & cold
        but one day wiser

mourning-
not my own woes
but the sorrow
of my serene, comforting friend.

January 23rd, 2003

Small Blue Poem # 2

The Sun peeks through layers
of thick gray clouds
and bathes me in a warm spotlight.

Says the Sun:
  Here is a small blue thing
  lying forgotten in grass and clover.
  Here's a weed
  to be plucked from a lush green lawn.

Now I've been purged-
you can gaze upon
perfection.

---June 19th, 2003---

Small Blue Poem # 3

Some poets
write a poem for months,
honing and refining
their delicate verbal sculptures.

The poet sitting at this desk
takes the faceless chunk of stone
that was his day,
takes a few careless whacks
with his blunt chisel,
then displays the scarred remains
and says "this is my art."

Last night, under a flimsy lattice
of glass and iron,
the poet sat sheltered from a downpour
with street philosophers.
words flowed
like rain and beer;
the poet observed in silence
between the glow of oft-repeated
cigarettes, now & then, taking hearty sips.
A bearlike man
in a three-colored kufi
flirted
with a stooped crone;
arid cackles escaped her lips
as his fleshy hand explored
her left thigh;
inches from her right hip,
the silent poet
drank and smoked and contemplated.

Shadowy men
appeared and vanished
on frantic, furtive missions, ignoring
the ceaseless baptism of rain.
One perched next to the poet
and sucked
bitter bliss
into his lungs,
then limped away
into the sodden night.

The poet wept dry tears.

One last wizened orator remained
to spew conspiracy theories
on a breeze of warm malt liquor.
"America
is the Beast,"
He shouted to the poet.

The poet waited for a lull in the deluge,
then escaped.
Two blocks north and east, he heard
a cascade of pure young voices.
They greeted him warmly, and pressed into his hands
a small meal
and a few of the supplies
of first-world living.

Gingerly,
he clutched his gifts
to his breast
as he trudged
four blocks west and south
to his home, a sturdy shelter
of glass and iron.

Some people
spend their days
refining the details of their lives,
varnishing and retouching
every tiny blemish.
This man, reading himself to sleep
under a streetlamp's glow
molds his days like butter,
greasy residue
clinging to his blunt fingers.
To those who love him,
he presents the crude results
deadpan, devoid of fanfare,
simply stating
"This is my life."

--June 20th, 2003--

Small Blue Love Poem

My two young sisters
gave me love;
its name that day:
     Yusef
     Komunyakaa.

The words he wrote
  seared the page like pain;
he wrote within
   ridges & hollows
    of my fingertips
    as my young sisters claim,
    "He is like you;
     his rumbling voice
      is just like yours."

Yet his face
on that book
is African, not like mine;
his eyes are wise,
not like mine;
his words burn the page
in ink
the color of eyes
I use to watch the world
through glassless windows.

Love is the shape & color
of voluptuous summer,
heat that drags me down
into the rapids
of a river made of sweat.

One slightly brighter summer,
a man with a face like mine
            gave me
                Neruda, claiming
            "He lives like you,
                he loves like you."
    and I watch, in the flickering movie
    of riffled pages
        his jetes and arabesques
            and I am not reminded
        of my own slow blind dance
        across the rubble
        of my sturdy brick suburban life.

I have mamas everywhere;
            their breasts
            soft as their voices
            as they croon love to me
            in the shape of Lucille Clifton
            ("She breathes like you;
                she sings like you!").

...and love on pages
        rains to the streets
        like silk confetti;
        I've met a thousand
        bright young mothers; each time
        I've shuddered
        at their beauty
        and gave them gifts of me
        so they could weep
        and paint me as an angel-

            they hunted me
            with their stone clubs of love
            until I became extinct,
            just another
            flightless bird.

Here's my quick wish list:
     give me Lady Lazarus;
     paint me in her
     pale pearlescent skin

      Let me cry,
       let me die like her;
         spill my ashes over
          granite-muscled gods,
          along sunwarmed walkways,
          and in the streaming hair
          of childless mothers
          who never look like me;

          grind my bones
             into ink
          so some unborn poet
          can write across
          the wide white sky,

          "This is Love."

15July2003

Small Blue Desert Poem

In the desert
 of my mind
  i lie awake on clover
   kissed by breezes of an inky night

Stars i see are only
      pinpricks in my darkness,
         I've never seen
            the light behind the veil

My morning sky
 is lit by soft pastels;
   rose & lilac are only hints
     of noonday sun's vengeance

Tracking across the sand
   (footprints snuffed
      by whispered breezes)
 i only crave
   cool drafts of water
            and here you come,
             with your rains
            washing land
             into rivers;
          your moisture breeds
          a rainbow of blossoms
          splashing brazen allure across my wasteland.

Your nourishing waters
 soon seep into the thirsty earth
    leaving my landscape
       cracked, parched & empty once again.

Colorless creatures
  who love the warmth of baking sands
  creep and slither
  across my landscape
  and i seek a paltry
  patch of shade
  and await
  the inky night.

July 14th, 2003

Small Blue Poem # 4
(Memory Wheel)

It is
ninety degrees at midnight;
sweat pours into the cradle of sleep
and I wake from dreams
of burning buildings
and thick black smoke that steals the breath.

Startled and bashed into wakefulness,
I watch the young and numb
stumble from nightclubs
into taxis and limousines,
bound for places I'll never see again.

I spin my memory wheel;
it lands in a cabin of reddish wood
perched atop a cathedral of stone.

In southern Appalachia, I'm told
this landscape is older than
man or God; I just nod
and swim in the peace
of crisp summer breezes
and a star-choked sky.

The memory wheel
spins across meadows of grass
so green they call it blue;
a small college town constructed of weathered wood-
its tranquil streets never tell me
if it's 1936, or yesterday

A gold chariot
carries me as passenger
through rolling Pennsylvania hills,
an industrial zone-
I sing the words on road signs
as a mantra
(Easton, Allentown, Bethlehem, Phillipsburg)

The memory wheel
tells me how I loved the road, reminds me
tonight I'm grounded,
stuck on seventeenth street
watching young drunks
and remembering other roads.

[At twenty-one, celebrating with Stoly on ice,
chased by
golden tequila, shot after shot,
year after year-
there've been a few pit stops, oil-changes
& respites, but after small pauses,
I careened toward the crash
that brought me
to this moment

at the edge of precipice
loftier than an Appalachian peak.]

I once stood still and could see
Tennessee in the smoky distance;
from where I stand tonight, I can see only
the flames that haunt my dreams.

(June 26th, 2003)

Small Blue Poem # 10
(December Dream)

in my dream
i dance with you
on a stage
of a star-choked sky,
   our supple twists and turns
                  applauded
   by an audience of angels.

my dream is served
   with sips of gin
   and puffs
   from a solitary cigarette;
   my sky
      holds no stars;
         only
         streetlights' glare.

in my dream
   i stand on a broad bright stage
   and spin my words into the air
   to be received
            by an adoring throng
   where every face looks like yours.

my dream
   fades
      to stark cold daylight,
            swept away
            like wisps of mist
            by a raucous jostling crowd
            where every face
               looks through me,

and those who look like you
see me is just another
speck of dust.

--December 31st, 2003—

Small Blue Autumn Poem

they are so lovely
    as they fall around me,
        brittle slivers
        of russet, orange, and gold,
        each one a herald
            of frost and fatal breezes.

this is a season
  when live things perish
      like those leaves,
          once so green and vital,
          now resplendent in the vibrant hues
        of their bones.

soon, the trees
  will drape their lacy limbs
      with ivory robes of snow.

my skin will crack
      under the weight of a north wind
      as i trudge toward distant destiny;
      whether its warm green spring
        of the fate
          of those lovely leaves.

10/17/03

1981

She is
marvelously fragile,
a blinding bundle of light
clutched tightly in a young girl's arms,
a tremulous soft and round
package of chocolate eyes
and caramel skin.
Her warbling cry
tells the girl and me
our lives are not our own;
they now belong to her.

Hectic high school corridors
are left far behind
as this young girl and I
step hand in hand
into a new world, vast and terrifying.

The sudden family in this room
emits a glow
which dances, shivers, trembles
like a candle's flare;
she
is the flickering light.

Here we sit,
almost a woman,
almost a man;
the girl passes our treasure
to my reluctant arms;
her filmy weight
nearly enough
to break our backs.

My clumsy hands
hold her securely
and I stare into her eyes,
opened for the first time yesterday
yet already as old as time;
in her calm gaze, I find trust
and imagine love.

Long years later, as the child I was
has grown slightly,
and that small bundle of everything
has been transformed into a woman,
tall, strong and wise.
I stand at the brink of eternity
then turn away;
my life is not my own;
it belongs to her.

June 8th, 2003

26 Hours (Brenna Poem ii)

At moments i was
    intoxicated by her trust in me
        as i led her, by her warm hand
          on a tour
      of the subterranean landscape
          where i live.

I watched her face (pensive & delighted)
    as she read story of my life
        page by pain-etched page
    & then i brought her around
        to meet some of the characters.

She listened as Gloria
    (cradling a big strong beer
      like a child)
    told a history
      of slights & failures.
Gloria mistook her
    for another visitor
      from another world
        but, still, not knowing who she is,
      accepted her.

Michael,
    thin and worn as always,
        told tales of police, always on his case,
          just because
          he lives out here
        with me.

My visitor listened
    with rapt sympathy.

Larry
   (housemate & confidante for me)
  gave her a dose of wry
            bitterness-
         not the only mixture
            from his pharmacy-

later, she told me
      "Oh, what cool friends you have..."

It's funny that i never think of
            the faces in my life in this way
         except through the wide eyes of a visitor
               from another world.

It's funny how she learned to respect
            the ragged stranger
               on the corner
                  cup in hand
                     bumming change
because, for an hour, she glimpsed
      the cold stares
         meant for him.

Twenty-six hours after our first meeting
         she left
            transformed; i left
            intoxicated
               by her trust in me.

July 23rd, 2002

Human Nature

I know an angel
  who washes me
   in waves of comfort;
   her cool voice
   is a salve to soothe all my hurts.
Though I sleep with
  bitter breezes of wintry nights,
  dreams of her
  wrap me
  in soft blankets of warmth.

I know a devil
  who casts me out
   from a cocoon of comfort
   into stinging rains;
  her cold voice
  is a thorny branch
   which lashes me
    until I am washed in blood.
When I lie awake at night,
wounded by the violence in her glance.
  I ponder
   this imp and angel
    stirred and blended
     in the cauldron
      of human nature.

---11/14--2003,@Miriam's Kitchen

Ink-Stained Madonna

She sits
in her darkened room
at her writing table
scribbling dreams
& regrets

Her blunt fingers
are tinted black & blue
from pain
and the torturous task

of bringing it to life
in words swollen
with history

"This is my life,"
she cries, with the voice of her softly scratching pen

The rags
that drape her wizened form
are remnants
of silken finery
that adorned her
at a time when she was honored, blessed
& loved

Now, love
filters down to her in creeping stealth
in a muted, halting voice
on a telephone
cradled in trembling fingers
or

in dusty letters,
grimy, creased, and smudged
by the unforgiving
flow of years

And still, she writes
(her trembling pen,
silently screaming
"this is my sorrow,
please listen!")

Her once-comely face
is now worn & battered

her pages
are blotched & splattered
with the black blood
of her exertions

Shame & innocence
flow from her blunt fingers
in her darkened room
at her writing table
as one more inky night
flows around her
oblivious, indifferent
to the torrent of anguish
pouring from those fingers

22 April 02

Independence

They found me
in the midst of my coldest, cruelest winter;
lost, adrift, alone
a nameless face with no story.

They found a story in my life
and invited me to share
before crowds of bright young faces
who cheered when they learned
who I was.

Sudden fame
coddled me among hotel white sheets
and warmth that banished the chill
seeping through my bones.

Meals in restaurants
featured conversations
about the wonder I was;
my story, couched in deftly
sculpted words
was carried cross-country
in cars, trains & jumbo jets;
on radio airwaves
and stark black ink on newsprint,
studied carefully
in homes, on campuses
I've never seen.

Then came an April day,
all cold and damp
when independence found me.

The army of mothers
who'd nurtured me
found a seam, a crack, a yawning gap
in my story;
the demons who haunted my lonely nights
had been revealed.

One childless mother
sat in judgment,
her steel-rimmed eyes
gazing coldly
at the monster within the angel
I once was.

One manicured finger
pointed my footsteps to a door
back to the snowy wasteland
of my coldest winter.

Tonight, all calendars
read summer
and rainbow pinwheels
splash across my sky.

The fireworks within my belly
are made of glass shards,
bitter iodine
and cheap vodka;
all fail
to ease the chill
of unwanted
independence.

Communion

A journey
of three thousand miles
ended here for them;
my journey covered
only a mile or so
of familiar urban streets.

We shared a feast,
prepared by them, a prelude
to cozy hours
of conversation.

Sudden intimacy
enveloped us; were we all
total strangers yesterday?
George and I
had nothing to offer
but our lives;
our humble offerings
were accepted
with majestic grace.

Quiet laughing hours of the evening
rolled on; while outside,
snow fell gently;
men like George and me
felt the damp and chill.

Sudden friendship warmed the room;
a sudden presence filled my heart;
a God I'd turned away from
gazed at me with eyes filled with love,
eyes that shone
from nine young faces.

Nine voices told me sacred words-
"you are not a stranger here."

After the soft eternity of the evening,
George and I
walked away
into the cold black night.

Our boots
slipped and slid
on last week's snow,
but for us
winter's chill
was a far-off memory;
we walked in warmth
from the glow
we'd just left behind.

~~~~~February 28th, 2003~~~~~

Tale of Joseph

his words
  drop down
  like dazzling
  silver beads;
they are
  coarse & angular,
    smooth & polished gems,
stacked and mortared
into towering obelisks;
joseph's words
    were forged by years of nightly drama
    played out on the frenzied stage
    of harlem streets & alleys

  where
addicts' lust & hunger
  consumed all,
    among bare concrete walls,
  in jittery candlelight

rogue males
flashing
bright cocaine eyes
  tangled in the heat & dark
  of joseph's world;
he surveyed the carnival
from a throne
of scuffed leather
and cold indifference,
watching his own self-sabotage
with scalpel-keen
vision

joseph has escaped
  his bitter underworld
  of memories
  to land
here
  at the base
of soft concrete stairs

he steals knowledge
from the privacy of predawn doorways;
  wisdom pilfered and collected
  is fuel for flames
licking
from his lips

seeds of chaos
  planted in fruitful soil between his ears
  bloom
  into castles of
  hard
  torrential
words,
  now ensnared in sheaves of
  fondly tended
yellowed pages
  the fragile leaves
  drip with vinegar;
  they curl & blacken
from lingering embers
  left over
  from joseph's molten core.

October 25th, 2002

White

Lonely

  silent

    phosphorescent night

all my vision captures
  is a sea of crystal white.

  Downtown towers
   are frost-crusted islands;
    an occasional pair of headlights
     sweeps an unsteady course
      along
       an alabaster river
       which was once
       17th Street.

Today
  all shops were shuttered
(windows bearing
  white placards- closed, sealed shut for this day)
I heard the swish & crunch
  of cross-country skis
  plying streets of this southern city.

Tonight brings
  soft sting of sleet
  along my cheeks
(and oh, the trees
  look so lovely
   in their ivory robes).

Milky dawn
    rises above
      crystal urban wilderness-
I see, at least, morning papers
are written, printed, and delivered;
    front-page headline reads
    "Area closed
      due to winter storm"

and a southern city slumbers
under its white blanket.
    I wake and rise,
    brittle fingers
      struggle
    with ice-coated
    sheets of wool
    as I pack up
    and trudge along
    K Street
    (a stream of frozen whitecaps)
    to a place of light and warmth.

February 18th, 2003

Chicken Soup

Mama offers
homemade chicken soup
and questions about
the cost of clothing in my city.

I feel great warmth in this room,
which is filled with signs of bustle
and of relaxation;
a Lego-sculpted robot
stands sentinel on a coffee table
while black, blue and crimson
plastic soldiers
march across a board game.

This latest batch
of volunteers
marched across my city
stacking boxes, clearing littered streams,
making salads
worth acres of green fields,
serving
life-sustaining lunch
to a legion of the hungry,
hopeful or desperate.

The room is silent
except for softly scratching
pens on pages
recording memories,
vivid and poignant,
of good works done
across my city.

My own pen struggles to recreate
the wealth of affection
tinged with awe
flowing from my heart.

I've spent many hours in this room
with many silent writing volunteers;
strangers yesterday, friends
for these moments-

yet at this moment,
I am a child
with a loving Mama
offering
homemade chicken soup.

June 10th, 2005, @the Pilgrimage

Welcome

Hints of spring

fall on 22nd street;

the air is soft;

last week's snow has melted.

Even as winter fades,

I seek places of warmth

and here I am

    sharing soup and sandwiches

    with new found friends.

Most faces here are unfamiliar

but they hold openness

    and joy

    I've seen on many nights

    when winter chills

    gripped the air outside

    and warmth flowed within.

This night is just like the one

a year ago

when they had come a thousand miles

to my city

    to learn, to serve;

and I came to them

    to learn from them

    and to serve them.

Most of my days and evenings

are so different now;

I go home each night

to my four-walled cocoon;

I cook each meal

in my own kitchen-

polished surfaces

of stove, pots and pans

reflect my smiles of joy.

I'm lulled to sleep each night

by a window of white paper

adorned

with images drawn

by loving, careful hands.

This evening

holds an echo

of a night when I had no cocoon,

no bed or kitchen;

I watch as

images take form on a window

of blank white paper

adorned by careful, patient hands.

Most faces here are new to me,

but the warmth, joy and welcome

are as familiar

as last year.

March 18th, 2005,

@ the Pilgrimage

Seventh Floor

Through the window
of my TV screen,
I watch the wide blue world
where a legion of lives
are washed away
in a divine heartbeat;
where bullet-studded bodies fall
in desert wars and on shadowed streets,
where my grand and bleeding city
sits stilled and stifled
waiting for a coronation.

I click the window into darkness;
up here on the seventh floor,
there is no war,
there is no peace,
there is no
such thing as music.

You, at the other end
of my pen,
don't hear my silence;
I hear nothing else.

I once wove
scraps and swatches
of a life on concrete
into tapestries;
one hundred days
of comfort on the seventh floor
have woven a shroud;
beneath, I sleep through winter,
my blood flowing
slow and treacly
with the chill.

My pen lies
as still and useless
as the fingers which held it.

I've built a prison
out of spider lace, and climbed within
to await a thaw.

You, on the other side
of my voice,
might hear my rustling, restless stillness.
you might hope, with me
for a spring
when my pen
will sing,
bringing music
to the seventh floor.

17 January 2005

Elegy

It is finally
tomorrow;
I sit here and
wish for whiskey,
yearn for the silken solace
of yesterday, wonder
how I'll face all these thousands
of tomorrows.

I finger
crisp black edges around my dreams
and wonder
why the widow's weeds?
No one I love
has died;
I've spent my
   stormtossed years
   looking for mothers in the eyes
   of comely strangers,
yet they are nomads,
always seeking deserts
to anoint with their nourishing floods,
to build oases.

She was not some lover
telling me
   our romance had flared and failed;
   growing my life out stones and weeds
was her work,
   done nine to five,
   under contract;
   I was only a thick blue file
   weighing down her days.

Life continues
into this bleak tomorrow,
but we did some quality work-

I filled out forms into her ears,
lifting prayers to the gods of sustenance;
the answers now clutter my refrigerator
and kitchen cabinets.

In between,
I handed her
all my sorrows and secrets,
my whole being;
she gave the whole mess back
packed in an ark of gold.

On that final yesterday,
we struggled through our fare-thee-well—
words of sorrow, words of praise;
she sealed it with a quick embrace
and I thought
"she has never touched me
quite like this;
 this hones the ache and sting."

I wandered out of our life together
into sharp sunlight,
kicking drifts of crunchy leaves,
dreading tomorrow.

Tomorrow,
I'll put on my suit and go to work,
   look at the new one
with business eyes,
pray to more gods
with incantations
sealed in long white envelopes.

I'll come home,
wish for whiskey,
settle for water
and fondle
one year of history
adorned
with crisp black edges.

9 December 2004

Sweet Sorrow

Our December meeting
was as chilly as the season;
my veins were filled with winter,
like ice crystals
freezing me from within.

I was like a night flower, petals snapped shut
against the light;
with slow patience, you poured warmth on me,
leaving me open, and accepting.

You led me out of winter into warm green spring,
thawing the crystals in my veins.

Together, we built my home
through hours in offices and waiting rooms.
Each week, you rode the urban miles to work;
I'd splash my troubles across your desk,
faintly asking
"help."

The home we built for me
is warm and cozy;
it's a place where winter seems far away

but

December has returned
and soon, you'll fly away
to mend other broken lives.

I'll still be sheltered
in the warmth you gave me
but I'll be a little more
alone.

Other hands will handle
the paperwork, which sustains my life;
I'll still make weekly journeys
to the sanctuary where you found me,
but winter
will return.

December 1st, 2004, for Wendy.

Holiday

The day begins with a teapot's yowl
and continues in peace
as Tracy Chapman sings to me.

Outside my window, rambunctious breezes
whine and roar, yet I don't hear;
I am lost
  in songs,
as I gaze
at love scrawled on posters;
in Kentucky, Maine and Hawaii,
families sit down to feasts;
their children
remember me.

While Cassandra Wilson sings to me,
my Masters ring my telephone;
I sit silent as they tell my machine

"happy Holiday."

Poets sit neglected on my shelves
as the death toll rises in a paperback.

I rise from my book
to make shirts and sheets
spin and tumble in machines;
I spend two coins on the daily news
where the death toll rises.

Outside the window, temperatures plunge;
autumn breezes snap and snarl;

I think of where I was last year,

when those breezes where my masters
and my muses;

I am grateful for this moment, even as
I mourn the friendly bottle
which was my master and my muse.

Evening falls gently
in this room,
as I gaze at my wall
adorned with cheerful scrawls of
            "Thank you" from high school girls
from Paterson, and I remember days
when I was never
this alone.

My Masters of today
have brought a final feast of charity;
I dine
standing at the kitchen counter.

The teapot yowls again,
I obey its summons
and sip the sweetness of the night,
while Joni Mitchell sings to me.

November 27th, 2004

Blue House (Wisconsin & Chesapeake)

On a hill above my city
sits a small blue house;
through my years of winter,
I'd walk past now & then,
oblivious to what could be found within.

Friends and strangers
would find me shivering on park benches;
some would weep for me; others
walked by, oblivious
to what could be found within me;
I was just a character in a scene,
a daily urban play
held in a globe of snow.

One friend spoke to me
and pointed to the blue house, saying

"Within, a clear cool spring,
leads to a river flowing

home."

Home was a foreign place to me, but still,
I walked to the blue house,
and opened the door, hand in hand
with the ghost
of three years of winter.

There, I met
the brunette and tiny
would-be
manager of my life;

we fenced and sparred throughout our morning hours,
she pleading, "please come

home"

Yet I couldn't let go of winter,
held in flat clear vodka bottles;
in the evenings of those mornings,
I'd sip my life away
to the song of frigid breezes.

A day came
when I stopped
struggling against the current
of that river
flowing home;
my foe became a partner
as we built a bridge for home
with paper and patience,

and hope came in weekly envelopes, all addressed to me.

Today,
I sit among my own four walls
at gaze out my window at autumn trees
whose colors no longer signal
months of chills.

The river flowing home
reaches the sea on this day,
it source, one mile north
in the warm room of a blue house.

When I go there now, I see
ghosts of my three-year winter
sipping coffee, munching sandwiches, and I hope

each one finds the river
flowing homeward.

7November2004

Art Gallery

"these images
      were constructed

        of tone,
          line,
            and tint"

-and a ridge of chrysanthemums blooms
        on a worn brick wall.

A still life of
      pots and pans
        made of stainless steel and blue ink

    accompanies the blossoms,
       invoking kitchen scents
         of tarragon and grease.

A man of tin
    strums a banjo; he stares at you
      from a window of silver nitrate;

adorning his wall elsewhere
   is a gleaming
     scarlet
       curvaceous
         fire extinguisher
           (1993, brass and steel);

take a few more steps
    past a silent audience of

      baked clay bricks, and

"intermediate photography students,
photographed at night
with a high-speed Nikon"

Stop at a mirror,
   passively observant
       (You: 2004: flesh and bone and skin);

you've found a home
     in this gallery,
----30October2004,@Loyola College, Baltimore, Mary-
land----

Two for Tea

Chilly

autumn sunrise,

a cup of tea
to warm four hands…

Nearby, Admiral Farragut,
stalwart
 among his cannons,
  gazes over a sea
   of grass and concrete.

Beneath his gaze, two figures
huddle on a park bench,
 swaddled in layers against the chill.

She holds ungloved hands around a cylinder
of cardboard, grateful
for a gift of radiant heat;
she passes her gift to him,
while she listens.

Her companions
have wandered off
to a sidewalk grate
which pours surplus warmth
into the morning.

She sips through the cup's lid;
he sips from the rim
 as she reads the pages of his life by dawn's thin light;
  as she listens

to chronicles of a life lived on grass and concrete
beneath the admiral's steely glare.

Blanket shrouded figures amble along adjacent pathways;
she sees each one
in the clear bright light
of his words.

Hot tea warms both from within;

the companions return from their grate,

  oblivious

to an autumn moment

etched
into two lives.

October 25th, 2004

Packing (Allen Lee 4)

Here are
Bukowski and Neruda,
Lucille and Sylvia
  packed away with Bibles,
coddled and swaddled
as consecrated voices.

Here are shirts
in mysterious indigo
and brazen crimson,
stashed away
for a journey to an alien clime.

Here is a life
boxed and bagged
for transport
              to a shining realm
              above an autumnal canopy.

I pack away
towels and Tupperware,
    pens and papers
and one scorching summer.

A valise is crammed
with memories
  of sultry evenings
with Renee in 409,

        and of Jim from 405, with
eternal grin splashed across his face,
chilled can of Busch or Molson
        clenched in his meaty fist.

I pack the yelps
and clattery thunder
of children who stomp my ceiling
and keg-fueled shouts
blasting down the street
                    from fraternity row.

Pack, stuff, stash;
my years have found
so many uses for Hefty bags
and my life has grown by the ton.

I once lived a simpler life
when my bags were packed each day;
  now my four-walled world
is littered with the baggage of success.

Pack, thrust, cram;
when I reach my hilltop,
  I'll gaze through my wall of window
at my new sunset
and riotous foliage sprawled below
just before I begin
to unpack.

4october2004, @the Allen Lee hotel

Falls

This had been my favorite season;
    I'd been a child
        who ran and leapt
            through yielding
                crinkly drifts
            of fallen leaves;

I'd been a man
    who strolled under canopies
        of brilliant russet, orange, and gold
      loving new crispness
        in the air.

As the season rolled by again,
    I lay trapped
      among walls of solitude
      and the heavy
        liquid
          betrayal of my own body.

There were no
    serene walks through a cosmos of color;
      I sat silent with sips
      from the blood of grapes,
        watching from my window
      as the trees grew bare and lifeless, musing

that this is season when live things die;
    and I waited
      for life's breath
        to slip away from me.

Today, the season rolls around again
and my surprise this year
is that even a life has seasons.
This morning I greeted the primal
turning of leaves from green to scarlet
and I sipped crisp air, feeling joy.

In every year and every life,
there is a time when live things
grow, bloom, and flourish.

Today, even as leaves
turn, fade, and fall, I avow

Spring is here.

-10October2004, @Miriam's Kitchen-

Forecast

For three long years
I lived beneath
the relentless drip of rain,

slogging through countless
miles of mud, and when I rested,

I'd write the chronicle
of this monsoon season
on droplet-stippled pages.

In the distance,
I'd see acres of sun and green
where people strolled in bright garb
of gold, rose, and crimson

while I was sheathed in gray
soggy garments dripping
into my muddy footprints.

Today I've found
the land of sparkling sun
I'd glimpsed
was not
mythical
or a mirage;
it lies as close as my next step,
beneath the edge of my storm cloud.

My deluge
eases to a drizzle;
a shy sun peeks between clouds;
one more footfall
will carry me

into gleaming light
and I can shed my shroud
of rainsoaked black and gray
and trade it for bright finery
I once coveted
from rainy distance.

---July 23rd, 2004, @Miriam's Kitchen---

Thursday Evening

A camera clicks and flashes;
  youthful voices giggle and whisper
  while a cry for silence echoes
  around the room:

"This takes concentration!"
  Bianca pleads,
      and the room
        settles into stillness
        as pages rustle.

Two days ago
these young voices
fired volleys of questions
after hearing tales
of three mystifying lives.
They wrestled with logic and perception,
searching for truth and wisdom.

They asked us three
  what led us to endure
  cursed nights of cold and hunger;
we three gurus replied
  "there are a thousand answers;
  a thousand shapes of truth."

Tonight,
  curious voices
  are silent
  as pens glide across
  days of labor in steamy kitchens
  amid the constant chilling voices
  of need and hunger.

I hope and pray
that these questing souls
find truth, answers
among their rustling pages.

---July 15, 2004, @the Pilgrimage---

Village

There is a village in this room
where young spirits from the different worlds
of Kalamazoo and New Orleans
share stories-
house-high floods
and nails scattered over city streets.

There is a village in this city
where forlorn and famished citizens
tramp through church basement doors
searching
for nourishing morsels of food,
for friendly faces and voices
which nourish even more,
for relief from
the fears of strangers.

All across the city
young hearts in this room tonight
have served life-giving meals,
have been those friendly faces and voices;
each one warmed and fed a hundred starving souls.

In the village of this room,
I sit like a sainted elder

absorbing
  peace
  wisdom
  compassion
  and harmony.

I no longer trudge, hungry,
through church basement doors
but in this little village,
I feel nourished, warm, and grateful.

April 10th, 2008, @The Pilgrimage

February Dream

Last night I dreamt
of peering through a window
of a gray stone cottage,
the room within, suffused
with warm glowing light.
Along the walls,
pastel ballerinas
stretched and twisted
their lithe bodies.
A fieldstone fireplace
held a nest
of crackling, dancing flames.

I stood,
paralysed by indecision
and desire
just before the welcome mat,
surrounded
by a swirl of snowflakes.

My left front pocket
was weighted down
with a jangly fistful
of shiny keys.
A numb paw
yanked them forth
and I tried them, one by one,
each one an eager tongue
that might fit the lock...

The silver one
slipped in but did not turn;
a copper one
was rejected, as sparks flew

against cold metal.
I twisted & tugged keys
time & time again
as warmth within
beckoned...

I tried a final key,
shiny and black;
it caught, slowly turned
and the thick oak door
creaked open lazily
at my gentle prod...

Then I woke
and brushed a frosty
three-inch drift
from the rough bench
that formed my bed,
from my icy body.

I reached into my left front pocket
for my ring of keys;
I found them all, except the one,
so black and shiny
that opened the door
to warmth.

_____February 26th, 2003_____

Lady CK

She has her moods;
they are like weather.
There are storms
that bring devastating wind, torrential rain
followed quickly
by bright sunshine.

Slowly, I am learning the skill
to bring her sun out.

But it is hard; my role in molding her
into the woman she is
was handled
with clumsy hands.

In twenty long and lonely years
she learned the lesson
that my feet are made of heavy clay;
she's taken the news
bitterly.

In twenty stormy years
I've learned the lesson
that she is not a goddess
on a pedestal, carved of marble
she is

a woman, mortal, weak, and needy

There have been times
she needed just to nurture;
I turned away, ashamed
of needing her.

and the distance I made between us
wounded her, and me.

There are times
when I think her strength
was forged by fire
and it was I who lit the match;
it's ironic, how that worked out.

But then, just the other night, when I held her,
I saw her as just a child
needing this closeness
far more often than I could give it
and, like so many other times
I sentenced myself
to a prison of regret
and my iron bars
once again
restrained me from moving close to her-
it's ironic, how this works out.

I reach out weakly;
my feeble hand
cannot brush her tears away.

February 1st, 2002

Mirror Poem

I hated you
because you kept staring
through my mirror
and I hated
your relentless upturned palm
awaiting salvation from your hunger

I avoided your houses
that stank of piss and sweat and booze
and sex, and the iron scent of fresh spilled blood

I feared your tribe-
stooped shoulders standing in soup lines,
bodies huddled under musty blankets,
men gathered with brown bags in parks;
I hated your calloused fingers
curled toward me, beckoning...

When my earth moved
I scarcely noticed the opening tremors
but then the bricks and stones of home
rained down on me like hail from hell
and a crevasse opened beneath my feet
and sent me tumbling into the earth\
and face-to-face with you

Now I share your hunger
and I look at the world through your eyes
my upturned palm
awaits your strength and knowledge

I've moved into your house
and, each night, sleep beside you
for safety and comfort

As I rest on benches
and watch the hurried sidewalk strivers
I comprehend why some hate me-
I keep staring
through their mirrors

December 12th, 2001

Touch Me

Touch me, once again
like you did just now
and soothe me

I know you wrapped your hands
around one of mine
just to calm my tremors.
Now, we both know, just one thing
is good for that,
but your touch did soothe me.

Do I touch you
with my pretty words?
Do I make you feel
young and lovely all over again?
With my affection and respect,
I seek to move you,
as you move me
with your touch;
I'll caress you with my words
if I can't help you any other way

All I need from you
is the vision of you beside me
enjoying my desire;
that, and your two hands around my one
trying to still my tremors

1998

Holiday Cheer

Holiday cheer:
a tub of soup
brought last night
by one of those random angels
in attempt to ward off steely breezes

A pint of something special
tucked away in a pocket,
to give the illusion of warmth
on this barren day

The streets are empty on this day;
the people I see on normal days
are invisible to my eyes.
They are in warm distant places
celebrating American prosperity

The only visible soul
treads slowly
weighed down by the bags and rags
that define her place
in prosperous America

She glances over, with a glint of kinship in her eye
and offers a shy wave of a weathered claw
and that is all, my human contact
for this day

There are times like this
when a quiet death
seems welcome-
I could drain my pint,
lie down in frigid weather
and go out with a smile

But, no,
I will survive this day
dying only in the inside.
My consolation:
the promise
that I'll see many tomorrows
that will be nothing like this day

Holiday cheer:
the way that angel
smiled at me last night
and the thought that, with persistence,
I can navigate the tundra of this day
and find myself, tomorrow
in lush fields of green

November 26th, 2001

Sea Green

I am
for now, wading in your tide pools
your ocean has retreated from my rocky shore
still puddles of you gleam in the sun
my bare feet tingle over
smooth pebbles and ancient shells

Ankle deep in you,
I feel a sting from a dying jellyfish.
It doesn't bother me, I am calm
in your cool water

Evening comes; a silver moon
returns, and lures your foaming surf
back to my shore;
I greet your surging wall of water
gladly; my halting steps blend into
a gliding stroke as my arms and legs
seek your eternal greenness

Beneath your surface,
mossy stones of brown and gold
glide across my vision.
The muffled light of a dying sun
winks at me on bodies of graceful gliding creatures
who live inside you

A city of shells
litter your floor
in a riot of shape and color

The urge to drown in you
pulls me farther from my shore;
stealthy giants with teeth
like steely blades
patrol your depths-
I am blind to the menace of them

After exploring you for a while
I am dragged back to shore
by fear or courage
I turn my back to you
only with regret
that my home
is not within your green depths

A brisk night breeze
and moisture from you
that still clings to me
chill my bones
as I watch your restless surface
from the safety of my shore

Some ancient signal deep inside me
tells me I must return to you
but for now, as I await you
I make my home on barren ground.

November 8th, 2001

Tired

i get
tired
of writing of this life,
the nights on bus shelter benches,
the rosy dawns, rising for breakfast
as one drop
of an endless daily tide.

i am tired
of needing tools
that don't belong to me,
of gifts that become curses
in the harsh light of dependence.

the fleeting satisfaction
of an audience
is an addiction-
when the cord is severed
i feel lost, lonely,
and alone.

i am tired
of relating the tale,
to fresh beaming faces,
of how i failed
to achieve the american dream.

i am tired
of waking to a mirror
that shows only me
(tattered tramp);
the face i wish for and imagine
is only a ghost,
a reflection in a darkened window,

some apparition
that looks like me
but doesn't resemble
the broken thing
that i've become.

i am tired
of being lost,
of wandering among tumbleweeds
aching
for something
to quench my thirst,
and of the void i find
when i seek something to heal my hurt
and above all,
i'm tired
of the dry throat
and sense of longing
and the words
"it might have been;"
hear me, be my
ear in the wilderness
as i cry out-
i am
tired.

_____

August 30, 2002

She Looks Away

She looks away
from the harshness of the faces on a screen
she looks away
from contemplation
of lives lived in a foreign world.

Could it be
that she's afraid to see behind the screen?
Eyes, upon the screen, melancholy yet hopeful
look through her
as if she were part of the performance.

She is shown
children at play
in the rubble of society's war
between the haves and have-nots;
she is shown
those a million miles and fifteen minutes away
from a miracle.

She looks away-
even as her eyes are transfixed
by the terrible beauty before her;
she looks away
from all these visions of want and poverty.
Perhaps she feels too helpless to help,
overwhelmed by the intensity
of all that
humanity.

At the end of the performance
she wipes a single tear
from the corner of a mascara'ed eye-
she can no longer look away-
she has been moved tonight.

November 20th, 2001

Pastel Ballerina

She moves like a willow in a breeze
stretching, turning,
until her slender form is transformed
like a flower as it opens.

Meanwhile, my clumsy fingers
struggle to capture an image
I'm not there to witness, or photograph.
My child, in a distant room with a dozen others
practices ancient rituals of movement.

This is art therapy in a sterile
psychiatric sanctuary
prescribed by Dr. Sara
to ease the pain of not being there
to watch and support
my nimble, fragile child.

Chalk-stained fingers rummage through a box
to find the shade of cinnamon
that suits her skin;
the fingers crease the paper
in a vain attempt to record
the flip of a ponytail
through dusty air.
Tans and yellows are deployed
to evoke shafts of sunlight
through unwashed windows.

Still, her graceful steps
are locked in my imagination;
the skill to bring them to a page
eludes me.

November 2001

Warmth

A stony winter sky
frames
a world of bare trees
& dirty snow;

last week's ice crystals crunch underfoot
as she exhales
white clouds of mist.

She craves
warmth.

A bitter morning chill
penetrates her skin
and on this day,
she feels
her winter is eternal.

She craves

a burning ember
blooming into roaring flame
to thaw her body.

She craves
springtime and the awakening
of the dormant earth;

she wants
the heat & light from a thousand candles
to dispel her frigid gloom.

From the corner of her eye
she spies a source
of what she desires-

clouds of smoke
drift
from a distant chimney.

She wanders
toward the promise
of a blazing fire

steam heat
enough to make her sweat.

Hope blooms within her;
filled with purpose,
she trudges through grimy slush
& breathes deeply in the frosty air,
heading homeward.

January 4th, 2002

Clear Gray Eyes

Her clear gray eyes
see beauty all around her
even where other eyes see
only misery and squalor.

Yet she doesn't see the kind of beauty
hidden only to herself
she doesn't hear
the wisdom and insight
in her own words.

she likes to say
'I can't;'
in fear of failures that never come
she has stood upon a stage
portraying someone's nameless sister
but a time will come, someday soon
for her to step into the light .

She can be seen, by others' eyes
blossoming, step by step
into the strong and graceful creature
she is destined to become.

Her clear gray eyes
see brilliance from across a room
but when her clouded mirror clears
she will see the pure bright light
that shines deep within.

December 3rd, 2001

Forgotten One

I am a forgotten one
though you see me each day
on random street corners,
and in the parks that are your playgrounds.

My home is the concrete
outside the elegant building
where you work each day
or behind the restaurant where you chat and laugh
and shovel down your steak & lobster.

Your eyes stare without seeing;
when you notice me at all
you see just a tattered tramp
troubling you for spare change.

You don't see the lines and scars on my face
or the wounds I hold within
in your world, I am discarded
like the remnants of your last meal
I am forgotten
like the chill of long ago winters.

Your vision of me:
a nuisance if not a menace,
a disgusting drunk lurking in an alley,
bothering you with my many needs,
cluttering your streets
as unsightly litter .

And in the rare moments
when you toss me
a "good morning" or random smile
you don't see the warmth that fills my heart .

And as you settle down to bed
you don't feel the lethal wind
that whips across my nest
of cardboard and thick blankets
stacked atop the pavement
your soft shoes trample every day;
when you slide into dreams of comfort
those dreams don't include
the forgotten one.

Takoma Poem

She says,
"I'd see him in front of the 7-Eleven
with a paper cup
jingling with coins, singing
'Please, some change
for coffee?'
and I'd drop
dimes & quarters
and a smile if I could spare it."

I listen to her
with a smile of my own, remembering
cold rainy days,
slogging to the store
for my evening sixpack,
and there he was,
bearded, bedraggled, crusty,
stinking of morning
Wild Irish Rose
looking at me
with hope
in his yellow eyes,
with one sad word for me:
"Please?"

He stood between me
and a door leading
to a dry warm place
with succulent feasts
stacked upon shelves
and an army
of gleaming bottles
standing sentry;
they tempted and invited me.

This drunken bum
  looked into my eyes
    into a place inside me;
    flames of fear danced briefly
    within, until doused
    by the icy water
    of indifference; the only words I said:
    "Please step aside."

I brushed past the ragged stranger
into my own sanctuary,
I walked the aisles, and piled a cart heavy
  with the grist of a life of comfort;
      sweetly fragrant
      loaves of bread,
        heavy shrink-wrapped meats,
      and six brown bottles
        of liquid peace.

Stepping back into the chilly damp,
        I locked eyes
            with the ragged stranger
            once again.

No words passed between us,
  only a steely glare;
    just five words burned
      along the edges of my mind:
        "I am not like you."

___March 13th, 2003, Montgomery College, Takoma
Park, Maryland_____

Colleen on the Corner

"So nice to see you, David!"
-and I was merely walking east on L.

She rose from her perch
betwixt Bob & Slinky-Toy
     rose into my space for conversation,
   she stood
    kissing distance,
     tight enough for me to sniff
       the contents of her coffee cup
   [bright bouquet of rancid fruit].

"I've found shelter
 with my buddy Jay
   and I've stayed out of trouble, except the night
    I sort of
      sn app ed
chucking my suitcase out the window."

  [street potboiler is interrupted
    by moments of bleak & sober
     lucidity, like
     "I can't stand to live like this!"]
So, she snapped, and
    "four fuckin' cops pulled up!"
My mild reply:
    "this is what happens when
    we chuck things from windows"
       -like I'd know.

She tells the tale
    three inches from my face;
    I note
    lime & lemon streaks
    amid the jade
    of her irises;
she staggers, sways, and grabs me, a dangerous embrace.

She offers
    her fourth-to-last
    Marlboro Light; I greedily accept.

"Still, I've stayed
    out of trouble
    except for one moment"
as she swigs
    from her coffee cup.

Slinky-Toy,
    face gashed from a row with Jay,
    holds his bottle
    tenderly
and Colleen
    ends our quick tete-a-tete
    with a boozy peck
    on my lips
    & returns
to Jay, Slinky-Toy, and her life.

February 28th, 2003

Gray

The colors
are before your eyes-
the violent startling sapphire
of cloudless winter sky;
crystal white of fresh-fallen snow,
pastel pinks & limes
of the houses in your neighborhood
chill-borne flush
on the cheeks of passersby

yet in the milky lens of your vision
all you perceive
are shades of gray-
you dwell
in a world of shadow

Shouts and laughter of strangers
who live in Technicolor
are muffled to your ears
as your world blurs
behind a sheen of tears

Gray
is the color
of life in a cloudbank-
your hands reach and grope
for shapes of sustenance
but can only grasp
the substance of shadows
and you starve,
fresh juicy fruit
inches from your lips

Your ragged fingernails
claw at your eyes
to scrape away
cobwebs and cataracts
the blind you to the color around you;
your effort fails,
more tears drip to your feet
staining the ground
the grimy gray
of week-old snow.

_____February 19th, 2003_____

39 (Perils of Colleen)

Aftermath
of a celebration:

she approaches,
freshly bruised, maple-colored hair
fluttering stalely
in cold morning wind.

She was 39
on the eleventh,
three months my elder;
on the morning of the twelfth,
she awoke
half naked in a grassy field
hard-by the abandoned bowl
of RFK, miles from home.

"How did I get there?"
she wonders-
suddenly found
with no buttons on her blouse
and a craving
for a cigarette;
she asked a stranger
for directions
to Constitution Avenue
He asked
"Where are exactly
are you trying to go?"
She replied
"I'm going nowhere."

Listening with sympathy,
I confess
"I've had birthdays
a lot like that."

[Springtime predawn frozen in memory:
I lay bruised & twisted
beneath the stone bridge
leading to Georgetown, a puzzle
in my fuzzy head:
"How did I get here?"]

Wintry morning words
outside a soup kitchen:
"I'm not really
a street drunk
but I sometimes found myself
with unremembered scars."

On the morning on the twelfth
she wears a borrowed trenchcoat
to conceal her body-
some of the guys at breakfast
snicker and sneer:
"I saw her
sprawled on a grate,
all her glory exposed
to frigid air
and carnal eyes."

At 39, she's survived
yet another gin-soaked night,
bereft only of
her buttons, sunglasses, and dignity.
Three months behind her,
I listen to her woes
with the empathetic ear
of a kindred spirit.

_____February 12th, 2003_____

Kindness

I.

Familiar sound:
clink & jangle
of coins
held in a paper cup,
a gravelly voice shouting,
"Spare some change?"

She always
wanted something:
crisp folding dollars,
a cigarette,
a warm smile...

In those years,
I walked the streets
secure
in the pedestrian comfort
of my nine-to-five,
warm bed, book-filled room
and the certainty
of many middle-class tomorrows

I gave this street corner woman
coins, dollars, smiles,
then silently exalted
my own kindness
and the comfort of knowing
I was not like her.

II.

Chilling sounds:
moan of winter wind
rattling
bare tree branches,
echoes
of my lonely footsteps...

and a gravelly voice shouting,
"Hello, friend!
Come sit beside me!"
I crouched next to her
amid rising steam
of the grate
that was her home

This street corner woman
reached into plastic bags,
pulled out sandwiches and cookies,
a feast for her and me;
my last meal
had been
half a hamburger,
harvested
from a trash bin

After dinner,
I slept beside her,
warmed by thick gray blankets,
clouds of steam
and her thick, soft body.

III.

Next morning,
she rose
and took me on a tour
of her world–
here's the park
where the vans come each evening,
packed with food;
here's a church
providing weekday breakfast
for those like her and me;
here's a toll-free number
where I can ask
a caring voice
for thick gray blankets.

Her parting words:
"I remember
all those dollars, coins, and smiles;
last night, you gave me the joy
of helping someone
just like me.

****March**7**2003****@Miriam's*Kitchen*****

Printed in the United States
215933BV00001B/50/P

9 781438 955933